AIRPORTS

For John & Sue
with every best regard

Kevin Ireland

Also by Kevin Ireland

Poetry
Face to Face (Pegasus, 1963)
Educating the Body (Caxton, 1967)
A Letter from Amsterdam (Amphedesma, 1972)
Orchids Hummingbirds and other poems (Auckland/Oxford, 1974)
A Grammar of Dreams (Wai-te-ata, 1975)
Literary Cartoons (Islands/Hurricane, 1978)
The Dangers of Art (Cicada, 1980)
Practice Night in the Drill Hall (Oxford, 1984)
The Year of the Comet (Islands, 1986)
Selected Poems (Oxford, 1987)
Tiberius at the Beehive (Auckland, 1990)
Skinning a Fish (Hazard, 1994)
Anzac Day (Hazard, 1997)
Fourteen Reasons for Writing (Hazard, 2001)
Walking the Land (Hazard, 2003)

Fiction
Sleeping with the Angels (Penguin, 1995)
Blowing My Top (Penguin, 1996)
The Man Who Never Lived (Random, 1997)
The Craymore Affair (Random, 2000)
Getting Away With It (Hazard, 2004)

Non-fiction
The New Zealand Collection (Random, 1989)
Under the Bridge and Over the Moon (Random, 1998)
Backwards to Forwards (Vintage 2002)
On Getting Old (Four Winds, 2005)
How to Catch a Fish (Awa Press, 2005)

KEVIN IRELAND

AIRPORTS
and other wasted days

HAZARD PRESS
publishers

For my newest grandson, Stanley

With thanks to the editors who selected some of these poems to appear in the *New Zealand Listener, North & South* and *Law News*.

Publication of this book has been supported by a publishing grant from Creative New Zealand.

Published by Hazard Press Limited
P.O. Box 2151, Christchurch, New Zealand
info@hazard.co.nz
www.hazardpress.co.nz

First published 2007
© Kevin Ireland 2007

The author has asserted his moral rights in the work.
This book is copyright. Except for the purposes of fair reviewing, no part of this publication (whether it be in any eBook, digital, electronic or traditionally printed format or otherwise) may be reproduced or transmitted in any form or by any means, electronic, digital or mechanical, including CD, DVD, eBook, PDF format, photocopying, recording, or any information storage and retrieval system, including by any means via the internet or World Wide Web, or by any means yet undiscovered, without permission in writing from the publisher. Infringers of copyright render themselves liable to prosecution.

ISBN 978-1-877393-34-1

Front cover illustration by Malcolm Evans
Cover design by Quentin Wilson

Printed in New Zealand

CONTENTS

PART 1: AIRPORTS

The inconsolability of airports	9
Brisbane bona fides	10
Lost in an airport	11
Airports	12
The true alternative to airports	13
Kennedy Airport	15
Air exotica	16
My first airport	17
Airport blues	18
Air rage	19
Air vendors	20

PART 2: HOME AGAIN

The very thought of you	23
Starting the day	24
The very latest defamations	25
A different country	27
A line upon the waters	29
This is goodbye	30
Facing the political music	31
A literary confession	32
Lament for a lost shopper	33
A new book of addresses	34
In the marketplace	35

Look at the trophy cabinets	36
The trophy cabinet revisited	37
The pleasure of sound	38
Memorials to the brain	39
Nothing to it	41
The witness	42
So much for your new year's message, thanks	43
A is for art	44
Patterns of play	45
Portrait of a poet	46
A new year's resolution	47
Poetry day	48
Letter to a poet in the wilderness	49
The road	51
Running scared	53
For Bernard Brown at seventy	55
The scoreboards of our dreams	57
Much talk	59
Ghosts and glass	60
The art of it	61
Rhymes for reason	62
A recipe for existence	63
In praise of whatever	64
The night ahead	65
A room with two views	66
A thirteenth poem	67
Wasted days	68
Preparations for the voyage	69
Trade secrets	70

PART I: AIRPORTS

THE INCONSOLABILITY OF AIRPORTS

Even the most desperate of lovers,
deluded by lust and moonbeams,
do not make love in airports.

Earnestly, grounded in car parks, yes,
and (by hearsay) at high altitudes,
but never it seems in that shadowed zone

of meeting, parting and transference.
There always has to be somewhere better
to go. Yet I have traced your name

in wine rings and sugar grains,
doodled declarations over the backs
of boarding passes, and seen the squadrons

of my words lift off from all gravity,
to be mopped up by shiftless clouds.
Airports are inconsolable.

The high-octane screams of coming and going
destroy those who have love on their minds
and wait their turn to be anywhere else,

as the names of great cities clatter
across the walls and our hearts must once more
talk themselves down from the skies.

BRISBANE BONA FIDES

I remember Brisbane as the friendliest place.
We stopped there, more than thirty years ago,
for fuel – the way a pilot would sometimes think
it might just be on the safe side to drop in
and fill up at the nearest petrol station.

There was only this one large shiny shed,
which we all strolled over to, for a casual stretch.
Everyone seemed delighted to see us.
People nodded and smiled, and didn't say much.
They didn't attempt to sell us anything

and they seemed to accept that we were just
passing through. In fact, I now forget
where we had come from and exactly where
we were going – just the need to make sure
the tanks were full then to move on.

That's the kind of airport I admire.
They took our bona fides for granted,
without needing to ask for paper credentials,
check our bank balances or rummage
through our raincoats or underwear.

The last time I was there was different
for all the usual reasons. The single runway,
cut out of the bush, had gone. In its place
was a superbly organised mess of concrete walls,
escalators and blind windows.

In fact, there were really two airports,
with a fast-train connection. But what was startling
was that the whole place actually seemed
to have shrivelled. Something was missing.
There was a vast amount more of less.

LOST IN AN AIRPORT

The longest wait I ever had during a flight
was seventeen hours trapped in LA airport
during the DC10 scare. We sat around, half-sleeping
and reading and stretching, but none of us could leave
in case a replacement plane turned up at the end
of our air tunnel – which the authorities kept promising.
Finally, they said we had one, and they ordered us
to get ready to board, but luckily someone looked
and saw there was nothing out there but tarmac
(a long way down). I heard the attendant say
into his telephone: 'You promised there was a plane…'
followed by a short silence, then: 'What do you mean
you've lost it? How can you lose a jumbo jet?'
Then a higher official turned up and listened
to the saga of the lost plane. He glanced worriedly
over his shoulder at us, and asked in a loud whisper:
'How long have they been waiting?' And when
he was told it was almost seventeen hours he said:
'They can't be Americans. There'd be a riot.'
Then he whispered: 'Who the hell are these people?'
And when he was told they were New Zealanders,
he said: 'And they just sit there, not moaning
and they keep waiting? Are they for real?'
Then, magically, the plane turned up. We took
our seats, and when at last we arrived in Auckland,
we all stepped out and something very odd
happened. As soon as we walked into the airport
everyone felt exasperated. People spoke angrily
about the way they'd been treated, and waved their arms.
Luckily we were simply too exhausted to riot.

AIRPORTS

I have spent more time
being bored in cars, buses,
taxis, trucks and trains,

getting to and from airports,
hanging about in lounges,
thumbing through bookstalls,

tripping over bags of bottles
and dodging glazed faces,
than I have spent flying.

Being airborne is the sitting-down
stock-still bit you do to fill in time
and space between airports.

THE TRUE ALTERNATIVE TO AIRPORTS

Airports are trick mirrors. You step through
and discover yourself in another airport –
yet one that reminds you remarkably
of the place you have left behind.

They have nothing to do with the experience
of travel, even though in the early days
people would visit them for the day
to feel the buzz of journeys of the mind.

They would sniff the fuel and enjoy
the agitation of those arriving or about
to depart. It promised excitement
and the faraway pleasures of open skies.

They are now recognised as places
to be avoided, except as pick-up points
and put-down joints in people-ducts.
They suck you in at, say, sunrise

and squirt you out at dusk. There is no
romance in travel. Even the old ocean liners
have been replaced by floating hotels
doing the circuits of harbours and seas

that no one should be seen drowned in.
They are for long-term trippers, not travellers.
Just as the trains are for indigents,
cars are for buffoons and neurotics,

and bicycles are for people who like
flirting about the streets in skin-tight suits.
The only way left to travel in real style
is to wrap up nice and warm, and settle

into a favourite chair with a first-class book,
a couple of cushions and a bottle of wine.
It is essential to put your feet up. This is travel
as nothing less than an art form.

KENNEDY AIRPORT

It cannot be believed. Sets like this
are pure show business. A horizon
of skyscrapers has been cut out
and pasted on a backcloth.

The skies are filmy pinks
and blues. I am just going to
stay here and stare. I am definitely
not going to try to catch a taxi there.

It would be like climbing up
on stage. It is out of this world.
I shall sit very still and wait
for Gene Kelly or Cyd Charisse

or Fred Astaire to come clicking
and swooping across the boards.
At any moment we shall all
be purring to a hidden orchestra.

I put my luggage between my knees
so that my hands are free to join in
the applause. It seems I have bought
a plane ticket to the theatre.

AIR EXOTICA

The brochure describes this isle
as enchanting, mysterious, sultry and alluring.
It talks about its violent volcanic origins
and brooding beauty. I think I know
what it's getting at, though the words seem
just a trifle too over-spiced and sticky
as you stand there, finding them hard to swallow,
trying to roll them around
on the tongue, together.

Yet the word that really glues my jaws
is exotic. I don't bother usually to dispute these things,
but the amiable man who waved us in through
the shed that greeted us after our arrival at
the smallest international airport building
in the world, looks very much to me
as though not a day has passed
since his last smiling
appearance on camera.

MY FIRST AIRPORT

My first airport was Whenuapai.
I passed through the old converted airforce buildings
forty-eight years ago. The aeroplane
was a Lockheed Electra and it took
four hours to do the Tasman crossing,
instead of the fours days you had to spend being seasick
over the wallowing sides of the *Wanganella*.
My lasting memory is that (to the astonishment
of many of the first-time passengers,
including myself) no one issued us
with parachutes. We were used to war films
and we knew that no one ever got inside
a flying machine without being able
to bale out in an emergency.

I don't remember much about the airports
at both ends of the journey, except that at Whenuapai
our names were checked off against a typed list
and given a tick, and at Sydney, when we clambered down
from the plane, we were all waved through to greet those
who had come to meet us. No one even asked
for my passport. It was so very open and casual –
the way international travel ought to be.
Almost half-a-century later, I haven't got over it.
In recurrent dreams I still catch the airport bus
in Customs Street, head north, then fly to Sydney for reasons
that are not made clear. The single thing I always learn
is that I am never going to get a parachute.

AIRPORT BLUES

There is no seat less soothing
than the front row at an airport window,
where you watch the planes lumber doggily
along their runways, bend upwards

into the lurch position, lower
their backsides and raise their noses
into the wind. The sight gives you pains
in the legs and stomach cramps.

Just as there is no seat less reassuring
than at some soggy table in the bar,
where you may exchange damp kisses before
your bodily assumption into the clouds.

Yet the most dispiriting part of it all
is the last, oozy crawl along the corridor
to the tube that pours you into the hull.
It's the way you also make sausages.

AIR RAGE

There may be some airports
that linger in affection.
Rare places we drift through,
without let or disfavour,
keeping perfect time
with wishes and dreams.

But there's always one
that hits the top of the list
when it comes to hate.
Some stewpot of officiousness,
offensiveness, exasperation,
wrath and resentment.

I won't point the finger
at mine. But let's simply state
that the angels it's named for
blazed down from the clouds long ago.
It's a site of burnt feathers
and fallen spirits.

AIR VENDORS

You visit airports more times
than you ever go to the doctor's.
I've clocked up twenty-six
in the past twelve months,

which is nothing compared to
other years and other friends,
who seem to spend most
of their lives bouncing a breeze.

Then there's the hours you spend
waiting, sometimes for fog
or loudspeaker excuses – including
the one that gnaws into your brain,

called 'mechanical delays'.
On top of which, there's the time
you spend getting there and back.
Altogether, you devote days of your life

to these vendors of flight-bound bodies.
Agitated in doctors' waiting rooms
I recite quietly and patiently: Think fog.
Think loudspeakers. Think airports.

PART II: HOME AGAIN

THE VERY THOUGHT OF YOU

At times I can almost see you
sitting down at a desk. You are writing
messages in invisible ink. Sometimes
I think I observe you smiling. Then you get up
and walk straight past me
to pour yourself a drink.

This is the thing I most like
about you. No one can take you
for granted. You are above all these
ephemeral things. Every now and again
I almost remember your name.
It is a sign that I must be in love.

So this is a poem all about you.
The lines have reverberations that can only
be found in the echoes of past occasions.
I am sure we must have met somewhere.
I keep hearing things about you
that have an oh-so-songbook sound.

STARTING THE DAY

You start today with a declaration.
It is something the birds
shall always believe in.

They take you on trust.
They take seed from your hand.
They sing to you.

I am new to this thing.
My hands cling to the wind.
I am blown away.

You start today with a glance.
It is jam-packed with words
I have hope in.

I take you on faith.
There is nothing to hold on to
except the sound of your voice.

It bears me away.
The sky is filled
with the singing of birds.

THE VERY LATEST DEFAMATIONS

I see that, according to the newspapers today,
someone is sniggering that you weren't quite
what you declared yourself to be.

Well, over the years, I've thought about the way
these defamations crop up, and probably
none of us will escape –

we shall all have to be kitted out in someone else's
categories, even if the collars choke us,
the clogs pinch and the nightwear itches.

But either way it doesn't change a thing.
You will go on mooching about my memory
with or without your socks on.

I'm not going to reinvent you, and I'm certainly
not going to trust the smut of those
who didn't really know you.

The living always have the final word,
which means the last ones standing
get to dress up those who've fallen –

until it's their turn for the same treatment.
Which is something that few pause
to think about before taking their chances.

The rule ought to be that we should not
offer the present our apologies,
or the future our entreaties and excuses,

or hope to outwit the truth that embellishments
help sell the news. Our energies need saving
for worthy duties, such as sleeping on charms,

knocking on wood and crossing our fingers
to protect the remembrance of those
we favoured, liked and loved.

A DIFFERENT COUNTRY

It was a different country then.
We wore jackets and ties,
even to watch the footy.

Everyone had a nickname.
Big men were called Tiny,
Blonds were Snow or Sooty.

Women wore fox furs
with beads for eyes.
And they always put on hats.

Well-dressed gents
in Queen Street often had galoshes
and sometimes spats.

Even workmen sported caps,
felts, bowlers and panamas.
Swanks went in for toppers.

We were Saturday racegoers,
Sunday gardeners
and Friday-night shoppers.

Weekdays were for work
or school. There was a strict
time and date

for everything that happened –
except train arrivals,
which were always late.

Beer cost sixpence,
butter was one and six,
telephone calls were a penny.

No one went hungry,
and the needy few
were supported by the many –

provided they weren't bludgers
or con-artists. In fact,
everything would have been fine

but for the measly morality
and the greyness, with every poor
bastard toeing the line.

A LINE UPON THE WATERS

Tomorrow we shall all go fishing.
This is the name we give to a pastime
that combines a purposeful activity
with the wonder of time's passing.

Possibly we are even going to mull over
all the alternatives and reach various
decisions based on the best prospects
for everything we ought to consider.

So tomorrow, or possibly the day after,
we shall devote ourselves to affairs
that may soon be made clear in the dream
of things. We call this scheming.

Certainly, some time in the never-never,
we shall pack our thoughts neatly
with our lunches and go somewhere
in particular. This could actually happen

so far into the future that it is not worth
rushing into. In the meantime, we shall
cast a line upon the waters and put off
our plans for what we've utterly forgotten.

THIS IS GOODBYE
for Eion Stevens

The man with the white glove
holds the corner of a handkerchief
to one eye.

A grain of dust has blinded him.
He is furious that we will think
he is going to cry.

He will soon turn puce with rage.
Even his hat blushes.
He is breaking his neck

to catch a boat that will take him
over the ocean to a place
marked X.

But first he must cross
a desert that is as parched
as his heart.

He keeps saying he must pull
himself together if he is going
to make a start.

There is an ominous cloud
that will obscure the next step
he must take,

but he knows this really is
goodbye. His life
is at stake.

FACING THE POLITICAL MUSIC

It is unjust that those who answer
political questions that no sensible person
would have a bar of, will sooner or later be asked
to face the whole ensemble of the past,
as some strident new conductor smiles grimly
at the camera and gives a flick of the baton
to ornament the staginess of the scene.

Facing the music is not the bracing experience
it's ever been held up to be. For one thing,
the themes don't always harmonise and the phrasings
often go to pot. The bit-time players in the pit
either don't know the score or they're all thumbs.

Okay, you mightn't exactly expect a repercussion
to tinkle and jig – and you should anticipate
occasional twitterings, badly timed pauses, discords,
and even the deadly thump of repeated beatings
on a bass drum – but what you would never count on
is the way the casualties of causality are compelled
to stand and stare down barrels of brassy instruments
aimed upwards at them like guns, and discover how
an orchestrated reappraisal looks like a firing squad.

Facing the political music is no career
you would ever wish on anyone you love.
It's something best done by those who don't so much
have faith in progress as in the proposition that others
would always do worse – people who can put up with
the racket as it hits a crescendo, then calmly
shut their eyes and block their ears.

A LITERARY CONFESSION

The plain trouble with oil paints
is the godawful mess that they make.
They get everywhere: all over the floor,
on your clothes, under your nails
and even in your hair.

Paints are greasy and gluey,
and even though they are great
to muck about with, they're not nice
to sit down on, or leave on door handles,
and they're nasty to masticate.

Words are a different matter.
Ever since carbon-paper disappeared,
writing has been a clean business.
Our letters keep to alphabetical order
and they never snag in your beard.

Notice how, after a few strokes of a brush,
you need scrubbing, whereas after a poem,
you're still perfectly spick and span –
painting is obviously for rough diamonds,
and writing is for gentlefolks.

There is only this curious literary problem
of where the smells keep coming from.
And the sordid bloodstains on the carpet.
And the sinister laughter. Sometimes, after
a bout of writing, I don't feel at all well.

LAMENT FOR A LOST SHOPPER

When I could be out and about in the shops,
purchasing items to bring me right up to date
with the latest trends in exhilarating high fashion,
and keeping the trolley wheels of trade turning,
so that everyone can have jobs and money to spend,
so that they can buy items to bring… and so on…
what am I doing, but sitting here on my hams,
writing these lines for no penny-pinching reason
that any sane and productive person could think of.

This is a very odd manner of passing the time.
Apart from the folly and indolent bleakness
of scratching for words, which won't feed the kids,
as the days and the seasons slip by, undermining
the fabulous passions that prop up the splendid span
of your life, there's something vaguely unreal
about it. It's not a misdeed, nor a thing you might grip
or define. It's more of an absence of aims and drive
and ideals – a kind of deplorable weakness.

A NEW BOOK OF ADDRESSES

Address books store the contact details
of our friends and pass over
the items that aren't safe to keep.
They are caskets full of bare bones –

the juicy bits we knew, or guessed,
or always got completely wrong,
were never jotted down. The characters
lack blood and guts and flesh.

But recently I checked my lists
and was rocked to find a host of people
who had really died. It was like strolling
through a cemetery. The syllables

and numbers suggested signs on tombs –
withered, dispiriting, out of date –
the skeletal facts had turned to dust.
The whole book seemed deserted.

So many of those I have known
can now only be reached in sleep.
They no longer answer roll calls,
but stroll through dreams at will.

Their names pop up, riotously
out of order and shameless. They survive
in a conspiracy of memories,
dialling the chaotic alphabet of the heart.

IN THE MARKETPLACE

My stanzas set off
with all the raised risk
and bold enterprise
of a capital letter,

only to collapse at the end
in a small black blob,
like the head of a nail
knocked into a coffin.

Sometimes I have rebelled
against these transactions,
employing lower case
and deducting punctuation,

banking on the eye
to make its own adjustments.
But it's the implications that always
strike a final balance.

In the marketplace
of meanings there ought to be
no short changing
of the business of intentions.

LOOK AT THE TROPHY CABINETS
for Michael King (September, 2003)

It is worth going on living,
if for no better reason than
to celebrate the distractions.

Just look at the trophy cabinets.
They bulge with curious tributes
and outlandish achievements.

Each marks an absurd objective,
which occasionally will scare us
with its lack of meaning.

The trick is never to question
our best aims or true purposes.
We should use our time wisely

by amusing ourselves, as
the distortions pull faces back
at us from the silverware.

THE TROPHY CABINET REVISITED
for Michael King (d. March, 2004)

The collection is almost complete.
Among the silverware, the totara tributes
have been piling up, though a few morbid geegaws
came wrapped in impudent insinuations
at the manner of your death.

So it's almost time to think about
closing the cabinet, and sealing it with a few
final musings about pure loss, simple sorrow,
and the plain emptiness of parting without
a final touching and leave-taking.

The heart's pain will pass, but there can never
be a cure for this bleak suddenness.
We keep remembering how we were at dinner,
and our special guest came late,
because she'd been held up by an accident,

and how we then all had our own stories
to tell about that grim stretch of road –
without knowing. And how, in the morning,
when the news finally arrived, it was as though
we had all been mysteriously aware.

There is no forgetting the curious sense
of exhaustion in the air, for everything
had already been talked through and there was
nothing left to be said – except
that whispered last: Farewell old friend.

THE PLEASURE OF SOUND

The woman down the street has gone;
the one with the violin.
It gave me courage each morning to hear
what she could do with strings.

I would try to place each piece:
ahhh Brahms, or ahhh Beethoven.
Then I would feel what everyone senses
in the rush that music brings:

that gorgeous moment of something
vaguely yet distinctly remembered:
the pleasure of sound
just before the telephone rings.

MEMORIALS TO THE BRAIN

I sort through the crush
of my files, and am amazed
at the industry. I had no idea
that so much got started, half-finished,
crossed-out, then stashed
in such negligent order.

A glance at the letters proves
a misguided diligence
I could never have guessed at.
How did these people
deserve such vaporous views
on dealings that wafted away?

There is also a fusty cache
of neglected manuscripts:
poems, stories and limp ideas
that all came to nothing.
There are whole books
in there, sniffling into infinity.

And what about the toppling pile
of writing that comes in under
the banner of miscellaneous?
God only knows how it got there.
I cannot believe that this mess
trickled out of my brain.

There is no excuse for it,
except perhaps that I may
have enjoyed the extravagant waste
and the meaninglessness of it all.
Now, it's a burial ground –
full of dead notes, bony bundles

of paper, boxes and packets,
dry drafts of great projects
whose shapes I no longer care
to be left alone with. Old stacks
of ideas, falling this way
and that. Like headstones.

NOTHING TO IT

There is nothing to it.
It is as sample as failing off
a leg.

How can two purple
be so hippy when
the nimbus

prove that so many
more passibilities
are avoilable

and the trogedies
get lurid about us?
The onswer

is that I have always
filt this etch of
friendshape

it has a naice shoalder
and stamuch and a great orse
and tots

so I osk mysilf
why should
I busk for

anythong mire,
excipt perhops
lore of it?

THE WITNESS

I begin to live in dreams.
The news no longer holds me.
I ignore the signs in teacups
as night enfolds me.

The eyes I meet in the street
tell me nothing I wish to know.
The facts I stacked my fate on
shuffle to and fro.

Yet all still holds together
and hope and trust are one.
I remain a dreaming witness
in the setting sun.

SO MUCH FOR YOUR NEW YEAR'S MESSAGE, THANKS

It seemed such good news
when I woke just after dawn
and there was this sign
written across the heavens.

It spelled out in giant letters,
glowing in ruddy colours,
like an illuminated manuscript:
'Today is New Year's Day.

There will be heaps of novelties
that will be good for you all
and number one on the list is:
everyone is instructed to be happy.

Those who refuse will be punished.
Signed…' And just before I could read
who authorised the message,
the morning breeze blew away

the signature, although I think
it could have been someone
called Rod or Nod or Plod.
So for hours I have been

joking and tickling ribs
and laughing and clowning.
It is beginning, in fact,
to get me down. Honestly.

I simply have no idea
how I am going to be able
to cope with a whole bloody year
of unrelenting happiness.

A IS FOR ART
for Jake

A is for Art
as B is for Brush,
just as H is for Horse
and Th is for Thrush,

and if you make paintings
of horses or birds
your colours and shapes
needn't fit to the words,

for paintings have titles
as children have names –
except naming a painting
is only a game.

If your thrush looks more
like a spike or a bike
you can call it
by any old title you like,

and your horse can trot
in front of its cart –
but always spell Art
with an A at the start.

PATTERNS OF PLAY

The players are in the pavilion.
Rain has stopped play. The clouds
have nothing better to do
and are now just hanging about.
The captain complains

how the forecast was wrong.
A result was there to be taken.
Our lives reach a standstill.
Our thoughts, like the clouds,
are held up by the rain.

Yet I gaze through the window
and figure out that whether
the sun reappears or not, there is
a poem that has to be written.
In all this disorder it clearly defines

how it also has nothing better to do.
Rain has stopped play, yet a voice
in the mind declares these words
in precisely four stanzas.
Each of five lines.

PORTRAIT OF A POET
for Glenda Randerson

It gets no easier to put up with the face
that haunts the far side of my mirror.
Every day this person gazes directly

back at me with all the effrontery
in the world, mocking my most serious
expressions, making fun of my attempts

to comb his hair or slap shaving cream
across his cheeks, and he is always awake
to my vengeful plans to slip away

and leave him trapped eternally in the glass.
It is a relief, therefore, to find him detached
from the mirror at last and staked out

on a wall. He must now, forever,
suppress the smirk that is just about
to sneak across his lips. He stews in a last

great joke. There is still justice
in the world. Observe his discomfort
as he struggles to start laughing.

A NEW YEAR'S RESOLUTION

Each time there's a brand new year
we ought to feel more confident
of our futures. With so many millennia
behind us the numbers are beginning

to stack up even better than they were
in the past, which was still pretty good
when you take into account the hits we took
as great chunks of stellar matter

whacked into us. Then there's the floods
and pestilences we've survived,
and the famines, and so on,
not to mention the other drivers

on the roads these days, and the way
some people keep looking daggers
at you. Yes, I think we all have to agree
everything is looking up – except

no one in their right mind
would recommend anything so scary.
Arrows, bits of masonry, bird droppings
and the wrath of God come from above.

So, Citizens, let us resolve to bound
ever-onwards this year with absolute faith
in some sort of radiant destiny, while keeping
our eyes fixed warily on the ground.

POETRY DAY

Poetry day never quite turns out
the way it's promoted. In the first place,
there's all this strangulation:
so many lines get choked in mumbles
or simply pass out in a fatigue of bombast.
The bandaged moments limp off to the dark
where they too get grabbed by the throat
and banged about in an orgy of therapies.

The trouble is that some of the best stuff
was trimmed to read well in print
and it goes out of shape when it's barked,
and although you still sense the style
of the thing you don't get the feel
of the way it sometimes gets tight-lipped
and you now have to try to guess what it means
by looking it straight in the eyes.

And as for the rest, most of it was hardly intended
to be taken away and read in the silence
that shadows each word on a page.
The slumped thoughts never get shaken awake
to rise off their lines. You may find that the best
thing to do is to wish the cause well and take
the dog for a long walk. You never know,
you may bump into a poem on the make.

LETTER TO A POET IN THE WILDERNESS

Thank you darling
for coming down
from your gum tree.

For a while I thought
you'd get stuck up there
and never return.

I still don't quite know
how you got yourself
in that position –

it seemed that things
were going along nicely
then, whoosh, up you went.

I only know that it gave me
a crick in the neck
trying to locate you,

and I got eye-ache
gazing into all those dazzling
dappled leaves –

though, of course,
it must have been a whole lot
more awkward for you.

Naturally, some people now say
I was wrong – you were never
up a gum tree at all –

you were here all the time
with your feet jigging
up and down on the ground.

I hold that they have
impoverished imaginations,
for what is the point

of dancing all day
if no one is going
to launch you

into the crowns
of the trees – and hope
you come back?

THE ROAD

The road he could never forget
was neither here
nor there,

across a far horizon,
through valleys
of thin air.

Sometimes he knew
its bearing
never could have been,

for no one ever talked of it,
and its twists
could not be seen.

Yet in a smudge of skyline
at the furthest edge
of his mind,

it lay as a certain memory
that he could not
quite define.

It was something to do
with emptiness – a path
without a name,

and if only the woman
he dreamt of would come
to him and claim

the hollow she left
in his pillow the time she
came to his bed

he would fill this void
with substance, and see
the way ahead.

RUNNING SCARED

Today's new fear is an earthquake.
Everyone is talking about it.
The likelihood of it licks your toes
then leaps up at you like a mad dog.
The shock of it is not going
to be at all pleasant.

Last week our anxiety was meningitis,
preceded by tuberculosis:
the old evil was back again
and we were told that everyone
would soon be turning
their faces to the wall, coughing

their lungs into their hankies…
And before that it was tsunamis –
yes, okay, I know – that was the one
we really collected. As it turned out,
the killer wave took fewer victims
in the year's list than a stack

of regular agents of destruction,
which includes cars, mosquitoes
and the fumes of cigarettes – which
is no consolation to the drowned
or homeless, or to anyone else
on Earth – but it does expose

the fragility of that aspect
of existence we define as "life",
just as it indicates our unbalanced take
on "death". The possibilities
of pestilences, wars and collisions
with the asteroids aimed directly at us

get shifted to one side when it comes
to reaching into our pockets
or getting organised to outwit
a threat. And we ought not forget
that people keep dying in their sleep,
in their thousands, every time

the lights go out. Next time you reach
for that switch on the wall, spare a thought
for those about to die. Some are not even
ready for it. They have no choice
in the matter. Often it all comes down
to a small flick of a finger.

FOR BERNARD BROWN AT SEVENTY

It took most of an entire lifetime
to get this far, yet there are people
half your age who are already

twice as old as you shall ever be.
The great gift of lasting youth
is to realise that it is dignity

that makes a feast of our years,
and there is, even now, an age to go
before time's tripes sag over your belt.

So, the gleeful child in you still sings
in the shower, and lifts his eyes
to the same blackbird that thrilled

your heart, back in the eternity
of glorious weather that was disrupted
by the secret services of imperative

complexities, which can be resisted
only by the cheerful cunning
of resolving that each day shall skip out

to elude the footfalls of the day before.
So, now, at seventy, you may undo
the ribbons of all our present times

and open up the opulent likelihood
that whatever, quite impossibly, is sure
to happen next, has already come to pass,

and therefore ought to be, at the very
least, taken on trust, and perhaps,
sometimes, even be believed in,

simply because it may well
have turned out a lot better than any
more or less plausible alternative,

and it could, imaginably, even tickle
a grey world pink. Everyone admires
the way you have always kept hoping

that all our lives might, at long last,
make a comic stab at, ingeniously,
accommodating the songs of blackbirds.

THE SCOREBOARDS OF OUR DREAMS

We had elation beyond pleasure
when, in 1956, the ABs won.
It just about made up for
all those strangled years
when sixteen men in green
always seemed to have
the measure of a black fifteen.

In fact, the rapture of watching
a raw-boned lock
come away from the scrum,
cut through a tangle of Boks
and score a lanky try
was halfway between levitation
and a side-splitting rupture of the gut.

Suddenly, the whole country
seemed to need a hanky
to wipe away the tears of laughter.
It was as though the glum
and unrelenting years of Depression
and War had been shrugged off.
We were a nation reawakened.

The best thing about the aftertaste
was that there was neither
sniggering nor crowing.
Oh, there was euphoria all right,
but it meant we were filled
with an inner glowing.
It was a time when everyone

wore black jerseys in their hearts
and minds. Our fantasies raced
up the scoreboards of our dreams.
It was more than just important to us
that we'd won. We could at last
move on to the bigger problems
that still had to be faced.

MUCH TALK
for Michael Sharkey

They do it like perpetual machines.
They gabble, prattle, natter, cackle.
They are unremitting exhalers of words.
They sweat, cast, weep and bleed words.

But thank God they are willing to do it.
Where would we be if no one cocked
their heads to one side and let fire?
Who would not agree, for instance,

that the weather absolutely demands
that banalities be poured over it,
that the everyday begs for vast elaborations,
that love deserves every blethering it gets?

People who talk too much redeem us
from having to think for ourselves.
We are all nourished by force-fed slabs
of rant and bluster buttered with

verbal goo and gutturals. The world
is a far better place for much talk.
Wordless minds are filled with wailing,
and silence screams at us.

GHOSTS AND GLASS

Your hand rests on the glass lid
of the display case,
and leaves an ashen print,
which can only be seen

in certain angles of light.
Shift slightly and the mark
ghosts off. It is as though
you had never been.

Sometimes, your meanings
breathe in the shadows
and no one has heard
a word you have spoken.

Yet the touch of your phrases
leaves a sure sign. Look close.
There is nothing to see,
and the glass is broken.

THE ART OF IT
for Grahame Sydney

Art that is,
is also something
that it's not.

The squirt of ochre
trickling down the cheek
to charm the smile,

the word that arms
the casual phrase
with wily implication,

and the notes
that shimmer
across the scales

are at the same time
there, yet assert
a baffling absence.

All the things that are,
are shadowed by some other,
holding itself back.

Art moves us
both by what it states
and what it might have been.

Art declares
what is by what it does,
and also doesn't.

RHYMES FOR REASON
for John Waymouth

The path of light may sometimes seem
denied, obscure or out of reach,
but a man and his dog will sight the way
on a morning's stroll along a beach.

The darker route is found by touch,
hands brushing over shell and stone;
there is no guide or sign to read
as you wander through the night alone.

Both lead to places in the heart
that must not ever be denied.
Light is the dark made visible
and darkness veils the light inside.

A RECIPE FOR EXISTENCE

The eye is easily tricked.
It believes what it expects to see.
Just as your voice has often convinced me
with words it didn't exactly express
and I could hear only the sounds
that were already curled up in my ear.

The mind moulds the world to fit
its inclinations. I am an intimate
of city skylines that leave no marks on maps –
the conurbations of the heart. I stray
their guileless byways and mazy squares
where deepest night is day.

The crunching sweetness of the breeze
as it sweeps over the ridges of tussock
is the taste of my dreams. I must consume
deceptions that nourish truth. I steady myself
by gripping rock-hard handfuls of air.
Nothing shall evermore be what it seems.

IN PRAISE OF WHATEVER

You ask me to consider the magnificence of mountains.
I cannot help but be impressed. Magnificence
is definitely the word. It suggests the grandeur of rock
and crag, with a slippery dressing of melting snow and ice.

I have taken in landscapes that necessitated quite
different sets of words and intonations. The view across
your cheekbones, for instance. It called for a whole
vocabulary of remarkable ohs and ahs. And once I saw

a moon that required nothing less than breath-held silence.
And there was this room with a carpet that stretched
in a vast plain to a distant vista of pale wallpaper and
    paintings.
It insisted on praise from guitars or woodwinds.

I have gazed at the miniature fingernails of babes and uttered
phrases I have been almost capable of defining. The exact
meaning of landscapes is the science of whatever. It is up to us
to record these things. You can sometimes taste the
    magnificence.

THE NIGHT AHEAD

As the years rise from the table,
wipe their hands on their napkins,
put on their hats and coats,

and make their skimpy excuses
before hustling off
into the hereafter,

I reach into my pocket
in order to settle the account
and discover instead

the tips of your fingers
brushing the lining of memory,
then gaze out at the lengthening

shadows of life's afternoon
and enter a vertigo
that is halfway between

slipping off an eyelash
and spiralling up a staircase
of smiles to a bedroom

where our kisses
glisten in canopies of stars
and time forever crushes

the night in its arms
and breathes our names
on its lips.

A ROOM WITH TWO VIEWS
for Caroline

He opens the chill window.
The road is empty. The hills
are cobwebbed with dawn mist.
The sky is mopping up a grey light.
Like dead flowers, last night's streetlamps
now droop their heads. He rubs
his eyes and looks again.

They have come here on vacation,
but despite their bookings and brochures,
when he woke he had no idea
where he was. Only when he first parted
the curtains did he realise
this is the place and the outlook
they have bargained on.

For her it was different.
Settling in was never an issue.
Right off, on arrival, she stretched out
on the bed and knew she belonged.
She is completely at home
in this room, although she has
never been here before.

They will get on well in these walls.
He has brought the intricate baggage
of a lifetime. Yet there is still plenty
of space for them both, for she travels lightly.
Wherever she goes the world
accommodates her entirely.

A THIRTEENTH POEM

Nothing should be either
too strenuously here or there
in a poem: it should have drift

rather than meaning,
and collect itself trimly,
yet command room to hint

at attitudes and moods
that strike the most chancy
off-hand style.

This is the thirteenth poem
I have written since I set out
on a new journey to nowhere

in particular. This seems
in every possible way to be
a good omen for its success.

The pleasure of thirteenth poems,
is their casual ease.
They stir themselves

in the morning with a warm
lazy yawn. They move close
to you on the pillow.

They are willing to take you exactly
as you are. They don't expect you
to be anything other.

WASTED DAYS

They accumulate from storms of dust
until there's little else to scan
but shifting dunes of wasted days.

As far as the inner eye can see
swollen caravans of frittered promise
hump to the far edges of the brain.

There is no excuse for them.
In fact, we were all warned of what
would happen if we allowed

idle worthless thoughts to litter
the breathing spaces between
the actions that define our finest

purposes. And yet I'm forced to say
that every wasted day accrues
in pleasure. From the first moment

of forgetfulness to the final
going down of whatever it was,
there's nothing but talk and wine

and books and food. Life is enriched
by indolence. I think of things
not done as buried treasure.

PREPARATIONS FOR THE VOYAGE
in memoriam George Haydn, d. 2005

Somehow, you raised the fare, bought a ticket
and got out just as the gates of the furnaces
were shutting on a whole way of life.

It is no longer an unlikely thought that nations
could do such things. It's still going on.
Yet it's you and your obstinate hopes

that gave us the courage to contend with despair.
Lucky you didn't return from your exile –
the baggage you brought here was filled

with tactics and schemes for outwitting the worst
of our fears – and how you shared it around.
I smile to think of you cramming those tons

of great times, good fun and high culture into one
scruffy suitcase – plus your faith in the future,
your stacks of romance, loads of sly stories,

sacks of ideas, masses of zest, oodles of pleasures,
profusions of dreams. It's a wonder
the ship didn't sink with the sheer weight

of the treasures you brought us – the infinite
freight of pure kindness that poured from
your pockets. It was a marvel

just to be near you. I see you laughing at parties
fifty years back. We all raise our glasses.
You have banished our tears.

TRADE SECRETS

They were sitting about in front of a fire,
with the tang of pine cones on the evening air,
and the room was warm with companionship –
then the talk turned to trade secrets.

A surgeon talked of his favourite shortcuts.
Alarming stuff in the ordinary way,
but amusing as they recalled how he'd carved
their dinner and forked potatoes to their plates.

A pilot told of how he always went by the book,
except when he found himself in places
where the book told him he ought not to have been,
in which case he did things they shouldn't think about.

A builder described how he solved his problems
by always taking the direct method. This often
involved chainsaws, sledgehammers and sometimes
a bulldozer. He removed obstacles as he met them.

Then a poet confessed. He owned up to spilling
blood and guts over his pages, getting out
of tight corners by leaping off precipices,
and sifting through mud to get at the truth:

it was the kind of thing no one really wanted
to hear; they were silenced and stared at their toes,
and blushed; they had not reckoned on anyone
taking on a dirty, dangerous job like that.